THE COMIC
DNA OF
LUCILLE BALL

✦

INTERPRETING THE ICON

ICON *(noun)*
From Greek eikOn, from eikenai, to resemble

1. A usually pictorial representation: IMAGE
2. An object of uncritical devotion: IDOL
3. EMBLEM, SYMBOL

(Courtesy Merriam-Webster online)

This is a TVTidbits book.

Other books in the series include:

Barnabas & Company: The Cast of the Classic TV Series Dark Shadows, by Craig Hamrick

The TV Tidbits Classic Television Trivia Quiz Book, by Craig Hamrick

The ABC Movie of the Week Companion, by Michael Karol

Sitcom Queens: Divas of the Small Screen, by Michael Karol

The Lucille Ball Quiz Book, by Michael Karol

Other books by Michael Karol:

Lucy A to Z: The Lucille Ball Encyclopedia

Lucy in Print

Kiss Me, Kill Me

For more information, visit www.TVTidbits.com, www.sitcomboy.com, or www.craighamrick.com

THE COMIC DNA OF DNA OF LUCILLE BALL

♦

INTERPRETING THE ICON

Michael Karol

Author of Lucy A to Z:
The Lucille Ball Encyclopedia

iUniverse, Inc.
New York Lincoln Shanghai

THE COMIC DNA OF LUCILLE BALL
INTERPRETING THE ICON

iUniverse books may be ordered through booksellers or by contacting:

iUniverse
2021 Pine Lake Road, Suite 100
Lincoln, NE 68512
www.iuniverse.com
1-800-Authors (1-800-288-4677)

Front and back cover art and design, including "WarholLucy," by Michael Karol; concept by Ronald White.
Author's photo taken by Craig Hamrick in New York, N.Y.

ISBN-13: 978-0-595-37951-4 (pbk)
ISBN-13: 978-0-595-82320-8 (ebk)
ISBN-10: 0-595-37951-6 (pbk)
ISBN-10: 0-595-82320-3 (ebk)

Printed in the United States of America

For Craig, my best friend and eternal critic (in the noblest sense) who has driven me to achieve some of the best things in my life.

"Nobody ever died of laughter."

—Max Beerbohm

Contents

Foreword by Rick Carl . . . . *xiii*

Preface by Dann Cahn . . . . *xv*

Introduction . . . .*xix*

Chapter 1   A Recipe for Laughter 1

Chapter 2   Lucy, the Icon I 3

Chapter 3   Iconic Moments in Lucy's Life: A Timeline 9

Chapter 4   Lucy's Iconic TV Moments 19

Chapter 5   A Red Hair-ing 25

Chapter 6   Lucy the Icon II 28

Chapter 7   Lucy, Meet Lucy 31

Chapter 8   I'm an Icon, Too 34

Chapter 9   Lucy the Icon III 38

Chapter 10   *TV Guide* Weighs In 42

Chapter 11   Laughter and Lucy 48

Chapter 12   A Clown for the Ages 52

Chapter 13   Lucy the Icon IV 54

Afterword 57

Appendix: Honoring Lucy *59*

Further Reading *63*

About the Author *65*

Foreword

WHY I LOVE LUCY

I have admired America's favorite redhead for as long as I can remember. Like thousands of kids growing up, I watched *I Love Lucy* reruns after school, but somehow a fascination for Lucy herself began to make a deep impact on my life. Not only did the Lucy Ricardo character make me laugh; it endeared her to me. It also sparked an interest in her film career and her personal life. How could you not fall in love with a great looking gal who gave the world a resounding smile her entire life?

As an illustrator who specialized in portraiture, I found Lucy not only a personal inspiration, but an artist's dream. Who could resist her beautiful clown-like, caricature face with those big blue eyes, red lips and, of course, that signature crown of red hair? I couldn't. I have rendered many unknown and celebrated faces, but somehow I always come back to Lucy. She's just plain fun to draw and very easy to capture.

I consider myself a lucky guy to have met the lady on several occasions. She was so real, down-to-earth and practical. She also seemed to be genuinely interested in what I had to say. She never gave me the impression of being a major star with a serious attitude problem. I have heard many stories directly from and about the people who worked with her. Could she be tough, bossy, and get in the way? Maybe...but who doesn't go through this when a hectic work schedule demands 100 percent of your concentration and not everyone pulls their weight? She just wanted things to be right and Lord knows, she sure knew what she was doing! Could she also be playful, charming and have a complete zest for her work? Absolutely. And it showed. Year after year. You do not become a beloved American figure just because you happen to be a good actress. Her mass appeal quite simply translated onto film and shone through the small screen.

Late in life, Lucy once called to personally thank me for various artwork that I created of her which appeared on a TV salute. It was a wonderful conversation and I even made her laugh for a few moments. Can you imagine hearing that deep, resonant laugh on the other end of the receiver? Talk about a switch of positions! I am forever grateful for this special memory.

Rarely a day goes by that I do not see Lucy's face somewhere; on television or the Internet, in a magazine article or a book, and it is very gratifying. I think she would be astounded at how the world continues to adore her after all of these years. It really isn't all that hard to figure out why.

Yes, without equivocation, I can easily say that I love Lucy.

Rick Carl
Los Angeles
Summer 2005

[Carl is a prolific, talented, and well-known illustrator, of Lucille Ball and other subjects, whose latest work is featured in the book The Official I Love Lucy Paper Dolls.*]*

Preface

When Michael asked me to write a Preface for his fourth (!) book about Lucille Ball and *I Love Lucy*, my first response was, "Well, I don't know…is there anything new to say?"

Then my brain shifted into gear. And I was reminded of a good bit I had that would be perfect. Life has a funny way of circling around on you. Some years after *I Love Lucy*, in the 1980s, I wound up as a vice president of post-production at 20th Century Fox, and Lucy and Gary Morton had their offices there. (Lucille Ball Productions produced Tom Cruise's *All the Right Moves* in 1983 while at Fox.) I'd see them a lot, and Lucy would always kid with me. A couple of times she'd come up in her golf cart behind me, I'd be walking down the street, and she'd yell, "Hey, Danny, get in!" Then we'd ride around the lot and talk.

Lucy was pretty serious off-screen. On-screen, she was a superb clown, with an absolutely magnetic personality, and now we have three generations that have come along since the show debuted—*and they all still love Lucy.*

Several years ago I was invited to speak in Norway, at the University of Bergen. They wanted to know about laughs and laugh tracks (in sitcoms), and I explained to them that we didn't add a fake laugh track, that all the laughs on *I Love Lucy*—the first sitcom with an audience, the first that was filmed and edited like a movie—were true. And then I ran some scenes of *Lucy* episodes for them, in English. The Norwegian collegians seemed to be pretty bilingual; most of those I met spoke English.

So there I had these European college kids watching *I Love Lucy* from the 1950s, sitting there—with about 200 people in the audience—and they were laughing *exactly* where we laughed 50 years ago: The comedy wasn't dated at all. Chills ran up and down my spine, because these college kids, laughing right along with us, were getting the humor right along with the audience that laughed during the original *I Love Lucy* filming. Whatever we did, we must have done something right, starting with Lucy herself. She truly is a comic legend and an icon for the ages.

Michael, I've never told that story before—that's for you.

All my best,
Dann Cahn
Los Angeles
September 2005

[Cahn was the film editor for I Love Lucy, *and the supervising editor for* The Lucy-Desi Comedy Hour *during the 1950s. He also worked on other Desilu shows like* Our Miss Brooks, Make Room for Daddy, *and* The Westinghouse Desilu Playhouse. *Post-Lucy, Cahn directed* Leave it to Beaver, *and edited* The Beverly Hillbillies *and literally dozens of other sitcoms, dramas, and TV movies. His feature film work includes the cult classic* Beyond the Valley of the Dolls. *He received the Career Achievement Award from the American Cinema Editors, USA in 2000. When we spoke in the late summer of 2005, Dann was producing and editing a 10-minute film honoring the men of The First Motion Picture Unit Army/Air Force of WWII, of which he was a member, for a celebration that was held in the fall of 2005.]*

Acknowledgements

Special thanks to Rick Carl and Dann Cahn for sharing their unique, personal memories of a lady named Lucy. Thanks to Marketing Evaluation's Steven Levitt. As always, kudos to my ever-vigilant copy editor, Saul Fischer.

Introduction

The year 2006 is the 55th anniversary of the premiere of a little sit-com called *I Love Lucy* on CBS. Most sitcoms from the so-called Golden Age of television (the 1950s), even those among the most successful and long-running shows of all time, have long been put to bed and forgotten [*The Adventures of Ozzie & Harriet*, anyone?]. Not so *I Love Lucy*. It is still rerun in dozens of foreign countries, and seen in our country more than once a day in certain areas. It remains the defining sitcom, literally and figuratively, of the televi-sion era. According to *TV Guide*, "If you sat down to watch all the TV shows in which Lucille Ball starred, shown one after the another without pause, you wouldn't get up again for ten days and fifteen-and-a-half hours."

Its fabulous cast of four—Lucille Ball, Desi Arnaz, William Frawley, and Vivian Vance—has become so ingrained in our con-sciousness that the phrase "Lucy, you got some 'splainin' to do" or some variation thereof can be heard almost nightly on some show or other, and the term "Fred 'n' Ethels" has become shorthand for a certain type of American tourist overseas.

Though an argument could be made that all four Lucy characters have become icons (see Chapter 8), the main attraction is undoubt-edly the redhead herself, Lucy. Simply put, Lucy and company are so funny, even the umpteenth time, they remain the sitcom stan-dard fifty-five years after *I Love Lucy*'s debut. There are so few other Hollywood stars in Lucy's league (only Marilyn Monroe and James Dean come to mind immediately) that her importance would seem to be self-evident. But why? It could be as simple as, "She made us laugh and forget our problems, and she still does."

What becomes an icon most? Read on and find out.

Michael Karol
New York
Winter 2005

1

A Recipe for Laughter

Take

1 Hollywood marriage, about a decade long, in which the husband (bandleader and singer Desi Arnaz) and the wife (B-movie queen Lucille Ball) have been separated longer than they've been together, thanks to individual career demands.

Mix with

1 strong desire for the couple to work on a project together so they won't be separated at all.

Stir in

1 savvy producer and head writer (Jess Oppenheimer)
2 ace comedy writers (Bob Carroll and Madelyn Pugh)
…All of who worked with Lucille Ball on the radio sitcom *My Favorite Husband*, and write to her strengths.

Add

2 sterling Broadway and theater veterans who can act, dance, and sing (Vivian Vance and William Frawley)

Combine Ingredients

Blend vigorously...

...adding a *soupçon* of vaudeville training (thanks to Pepito Perez and a trick cello) and a mastery of props (courtesy of Buster Keaton and Harold Lloyd).

Film

...with directors Marc Daniels and William Asher, using a special three-camera technique developed by Oscar-winning cinematographer Karl Freund and Desi Arnaz.

Edit

...using a "three-headed monster" designed for the unique camera shots and worked by Dann Cahn and crew.

Duplicate film and send to local TV stations throughout the country.

Prepare to give up any plans for Monday night at 9:00 p.m. EST.

Sit back, **relax** and **laugh your head** off every week at the antics of the Ricardos and the Mertzes in the immediate hit and all-time classic series, *I Love Lucy*.

2

Lucy, the Icon I

In *Lucy A to Z: The Lucille Ball Encyclopedia*, I quoted a 2001 *New York Times* report on the state of Hollywood Boulevard and Los Angeles tourism: "…It is easy to see from the faces emblazoned on the T-shirts [of souvenir shops] which icons still speak most loudly to the passing parade; Marilyn Monroe, of course, but also Lucille Ball, Betty Boop, James Dean, and The Three Stooges."

Lucy's iconic stature has been building steadily since *I Love Lucy* went off the air; indeed, she was one of the few stars who could legitimately be called a living legend while she was still alive. After her death, Lucy—whose face, it is estimated, has been seen by more people worldwide than the face of any other person who ever lived—has only gotten bigger. There have been two postage stamps honoring her. Tributes to her genius occur on a near-weekly basis, and it's a safe bet she's mentioned more than once a day in the copy of our national magazines and newspapers.

For example, on July 13, 2005, a search for Lucille Ball in the news came up with, among other things, an article on the Presbyterian faith, whose numbers included Lucy, and an article promoting the PBS show *Pioneers of Primetime*, scheduled to air November 9. Comedy legends gathered [July 12] to promote the series, including Sid Caesar, Carl Reiner, Red Buttons, Rose Marie, and *I Love Lucy* director William Asher. Regarding Lucy, the article noted, "The switch from live variety to taped sitcoms also produced what may be the most popular show of them all: *I Love Lucy.* Asher, 83, says they knew the show was good, but they didn't know it would last. 'When we did the show, we thought, "That's it, we're done with [it]." We never dreamed it would last this long.' Lucille Ball, obviously, was one of TV's true pioneers."

Following are various Lucy-related tributes and events, some personal, others national, which occurred too late to make the 2004 publication of *Lucy A to Z.* All were first reported on my Web site (Sitcomboy.com), and they reveal the extreme esteem in which Lucy remains held by the general public…as well as, obviously, the strengthening of her icon status. The gift of laughter is a powerful one, indeed.

07.22.03 **VH1 Chooses the 200 Greatest Pop Icons**
The cable music channel for Baby Boomers picked the 200 most iconic performers, logos, cartoon characters, and so on. Lucille Ball ranked number 4 on the list, which included television performers, the roles they played, hand-drawn wise guys (Bugs Bunny), puppets (Miss Piggy), and movie and rock stars. The top three were, in order, Oprah, Superman, and Elvis. You can still (as of this writing) catch Lucy's bio and a cool caricature by Robert Risko at www.VH1.com. Identified as "Television's First Lady of Comedy," the bio begins, "Lucille Ball—whose career in front of the camera spanned five decades—served as a pioneer for female comedians, as well as for the television industry itself."

02.18.04 **What a Character!**
Time magazine said "goodbye" to Kelsey Grammar's long-running portrayal of neurotic radio shrink *Frasier* Crane. He'd been playing the part since 1984, first on *Cheers,* for a total of 20 years. But the magazine noted that Grammar's feat, though special, wasn't unique. James Arness played the title character of *Marshall Matt Dillon* on that show and after it changed its name to *Gunsmoke,* for a 20-year

run (supporting character Doc Adams was played by veteran Milburn Stone for the same amount of time). Then, of course, there's the number one character portrayal on TV, Lucille Ball's Lucy, played by the wacky redhead over 21 seasons, five series, and 35 years (*I Love Lucy, The Lucy-Desi Comedy Hour, The Lucy Show, Here's Lucy,* and *Life with Lucy*). Neither Frasier nor Marshall Dillon could top Lucy, who started as a youngish married mother and ended up a widowed grandmother.

03.26.04 Elois Jenssen Dies; Lucy's Oscar-winning Designer

Jenssen, an Oscar winner for 1949's *Samson and Delilah*, moved into television working for Ann Sothern on her hit sitcom *Private Secretary*; she was then hired by Lucy to create a look for housewife Lucy Ricardo. Jenssen is credited with striking just the right balance of typical housewife with an occasional shot of glamour. Lucy's iconic presence during the 1950s is dependent on that look. Jenssen, who died on Valentine's Day at the age of 81, also did the gowns for Lucy's 1956 movie, *Forever Darling*.

09.28.04 Learning from Lucy seminar in New York

A unique design seminar called "Learning from Lucy" was held this morning at the D&D (Design & Decoration) building on 58th Street and Third Avenue in New York. Interior Designer Eric Cohler spoke about how, as noted in the program, "The First Lady of American Comedy, Lucille Ball, was passionate about interiors and a perfectionist about the set design of her television shows, including *I Love Lucy*." In his talk, Cohler explored "the subtle influences these timeless set designs have had on his own interior design sensibilities." Cohler has volunteered his services to help transform Jamestown, N.Y.'s former Grant Building into the new Lucy-Desi Museum.

10.23.04 *Mixed Nuts* is Published

The book by Lawrence Epstein explores American comedy teams in stage, film, radio and TV history, including a section on Lucille Ball and Vivian Vance. It is one of the rare times a writer has acknowledged the brilliance of this unique female team, and put them on the same footing as Laurel & Hardy, Abbott & Costello, and Martin & Lewis.

10.24.04 E! Airs the 101 Most Awesome Moments in Entertainment

Debuting in a five-episode marathon, the E! list featured a classic Lucy moment in the Top Ten: Lucy and Ethel, fighting a losing battle with the candy factory conveyor belt, as they try in vain to wrap chocolates, came in at Number 7. Savor Lucy's manic reactions at having to wrap too much candy too quickly (the extra bon bons end up in the girls' hats, blouses, and mouths), and marvel at Vivian Vance's reactions, for instance, as she misses her first piece. The two performers define the essence of an acting partnership.

11.30.04 Bravo Debuts The 100 Greatest TV Characters

Described by the cable network as focusing "its critical eye on famous television characters that have become part of the fabric of American culture," Lucy Ricardo was named the Number 3 greatest TV character, a nod to the iconic status of Lucy/Lucille Ball in the hearts and minds of TV viewers everywhere.

03.01.05 "Why Millions Love Lucy" Published 52 Years Ago

On March 1, 1953, only two years after *I Love Lucy*'s debut, influential *New York Times* television critic Jack Gould reviewed the show, noting that, "*I Love Lucy* is probably the most misleading title imaginable. For once, all the statistics are in agreement: *Millions* love Lucy." He went on to write, "*I Love Lucy* is as much a phenomenon as an attraction. Fundamentally, it is a piece of hilarious theater put together with deceptively brilliant know-how, but it is also many other things. In part, it is the fusion of the make-believe of the footlights and the real-life existence of a glamorous 'name.' In part, it is the product of inspired press-agentry, which has made a national legend of a couple which, two years ago, was on the Hollywood sidelines." The most amazing thing of all is that on October 15, 2005, *I Love Lucy*'s 54th Anniversary, Gould's assessment still rings true: the series and its star shine ever-bright.

05.15.05 **Stamp of Success**

They didn't rerelease the Lucille Ball postage stamp from 2001, but the Associated Press reported on this date that it was one of the Top 20 best-selling stamps of all time. On the list of the "all-time most collected stamps" along with "the extra income they have meant to the Post Office," Lucy's stamp is #18, with 39 million sold, and $13 million in revenue for the USPS. An Elvis stamp released in 1993 is #1, with 124 million sold and revenue of $36 million. The only other entertainer to make the list (not counting Bugs Bunny, whose 1997 stamp was #13, with 44 million sold and revenue of $14 million) was Marilyn Monroe, whose stamp came out in 1995; she's #12, with 46 million sold and revenue of $15 million. Lucy is one of a very few entertainers to have her likeness on two postage stamps. The first one was part of a USPS special promotion celebrating each decade of the 20th century with stamps featuring the popular cultural icons of every 10-year span. For the 1950s set, Lucy and husband Desi Arnaz were pictured together on a stamp honoring *I Love Lucy*.

06.24.05 **Discovery Channel Airs The 100 Greatest Americans**

While there were some surprises—Dr. Phil? *Pleeeeze.* Barack Obama? Too early to tell. Condoleeza? UGH. Mel Gibson? Shoot me! Hugh Hefner? A pioneer, yes, but one of the greatest? No. Richard Nixon? Hellooooo, Watergate anyone? Only President ever to resign? Tom Cruise? Jeez, I don't care what the guy is, just make him SHUT UP!—um, excuse me, that took a bit longer than expected. Ahem. In any case, there should be no surprise that a certain favorite redhead of ours made the cut. Lucy is in mostly great company, including the usual suspects (Lincoln, Washington, Jefferson, Franklin, three Roosevelts, Harriet Tubman, George Washington Carver, Edison, Martin Luther King, Helen Keller, and Rosa Parks, to name a few). Only the Top 25 were actually ranked, but for Lucy to make the list—she's one of only two actresses to be named; the other is Katharine Hepburn—is a major accolade. Chalk it up to the power of laughter, and a woman who knew better than almost anyone did how to deliver it.

Certainly, if there were a procedure in place to certify iconic status, Lucy would have made the grade long ago. These latest honors merely reinforce what we already knew: that Lucille Ball was a funny lady, that she's engrained herself permanently into the American consciousness, and, in doing so, has provided a respite from the often harsh reality of our lives, via humor and laughter, to millions upon millions worldwide.

3

Iconic Moments in Lucy's Life: A Timeline

These are the defining moments that transformed a skinny brunette kid from western New York State into the redheaded clown who changed television forever.

1887	William Clement Frawley born in Burlington, Iowa.
1909	Vivian Roberta Jones (later Vance) born in Cherryvale, Kan.
1911	Lucille Desirée Ball born in Jamestown, N.Y. Her impoverished, vagabond early life created a fierce desire in Ball to be surrounded by family and close friends.
1915	Lucy's father, Henry Durrell Ball, dies of typhoid fever.
1917	Desiderio (Desi) Alberto Arnaz y de Acha III born in Santiago, Cuba.
1926	Lucy attends the John Murray Anderson dramatic school in New York City, but is told to go home because she "has no tal-

ent" and mother DeDe is "wasting her money."

1927   A year later, Lucy is back looking for work in New York, and finds employment as a model, eventually becoming the Chesterfield Girl in a series of billboards and a model for Hattie Carnegie.

1927   Lucy's beloved grandpa, Fred Hunt, who introduced her to the joys of the vaudeville stage, is held responsible for the death of a local boy, shot with a gun Hunt gave to Lucy's brother Fred, as a present. The family is fractured and splits apart.

1928   Circa this time Lucy is felled by a debilitating bout of rheumatoid arthritis, after which she had to learn to walk again. Her triumph is indicative of a personality who will not quit, who will do whatever is needed to achieve her goals.

1933   A chance encounter on the sidewalks of New York leads Lucy to Hollywood, replacing a chorus girl whose mother wouldn't let her travel west. She becomes a Goldwyn Girl and starts her movie career with a bit part in *Roman Scandals*. Lucy sets herself apart from the other chorus girls by her willingness to perform anything, no matter how foolish it makes her look, on film.

1937   Lucy grabs her first major role, in *Stage Door*, and holds her own against Ginger Rogers, Katharine Hepburn, and Eve Arden. She has spent the past five years in ever-expanding small parts; after this film, she will never be less than a co-star.

1938   Lucy proves so popular with audiences that RKO gives her a series, in which she plays an aspiring actress named Annabel. Unfortunately, it lasts for only two films.

1939   In *Five Came Back*, Lucy's hooker-with-a-heart-of-gold character hints at the dramatic acting potential in Lucy that had heretofore remained untapped.

1940   Lucy lands the lead in the college musical *Too Many Girls*. More importantly, one of her co-stars is a rising Cuban singer/bandleader imported from the Broadway show cast, Desi Arnaz. They fall in love at first sight and will marry on November 30.

1942   One of her final pictures for RKO, *The Big Street*, co-stars Lucy with Henry Fonda. As the cold-hearted, crippled chanteuse who psychologically abuses loving busboy Fonda, Lucy silences anyone who ever thought she couldn't act.

1943   Lucy is featured in her first MGM film, a Technicolor romp called *DuBarry Was a Lady*. For it, the studio died her hair a blazing red, a color that Lucy kept ever after. Renowned MGM hairstylist Sydney Guilaroff created her unique shade in 1946 (see chapter 6). Lucy photographs so spectacularly in color that she is nicknamed Technicolor Tessie, as noted in a 1943 *LIFE* magazine article.

1943   MGM is not sure how to market Lucy as a star, casting her mostly as a glamorous showgirl or "herself" in extended cameos. While waiting around for the right role, Lucy is schooled in comic timing and the use of props by fellow MGM-ers (and silent film classic comics) Harold Lloyd and Buster Keaton, both also criminally underused at the studio.

1947   A successful national tour in the comedy *Dreamgirl* proves to Lucy she gives her best performances when stimulated by the reaction of a live audience.

1948   Lucy jumps into radio full-time with a successful series, *My Favorite Husband*. Head writer Jess Oppenheimer (a veteran of Fanny Brice's *Baby Snooks* radio show), and writers Bob Carroll and Madelyn Pugh, shaped the situation comedy to suit Lucy's talents, and she shined in front of a live radio audience. All of them would come to television with Lucy three years hence.

1950   Lucy and Desi, desiring to work closer
          together, put together a successful vaude-
          ville act and tour the country, playing live
          in theaters, that proves to CBS executives
          audiences would accept them as a TV duo.
          The go-ahead is given to transform the
          aural *My Favorite Husband* into the visual
          I Love Lucy.

1951   *I Love Lucy* debuts and is an instant hit. It
          is number 3 in the ratings for the season.
          For the next six years, it will hold the
          number 1 spot, except for its fifth season,
          when the popular quiz show, *The $64,000
          Question*, bumped it to number 2. Desi
          Arnaz proves to be a capable and shrewd
          businessman, hiring only the best, and
          with them virtually creating the sitcom as
          we know it today. Desilu's three-camera
          shooting technique is still favored by the
          majority of sitcoms on prime time. Lucy
          and Desi's insistence on filming the show,
          so the quality would be tops wherever it
          was viewed in the country, invented the
          rerun. Lucy and Desi play fictional ver-
          sions of themselves, the key being Ricky
          Ricardo is not a hugely successful show-
          business personality, allowing the wealthy
          couple to portray the fiction of being mid-
          dle class, the better for their audience to
          identify with. Vivian Vance and William
          Frawley play the pivotal supporting roles:
          friends and neighbors the Mertzes, giving

Lucy and Desi fellow schemers, and creating a template for all future sitcoms.

1953

In January, Lucy gives birth to Desi Arnaz Jr., while in TV land, Lucy Ricardo gives birth to "Little Ricky" on the same day. It is a watershed event in television, with an estimated 44 million viewers, or 71 percent of those who owned a television set, tuning in.

1954

On June 28, Lucy and Desi celebrate the filming of the 100th *I Love Lucy* episode. *Time* magazine reported that 50 million people, or one-third of the U.S. population, tuned in every Monday to watch the show. Jess Oppenheimer explained the reason behind the show's success: "The best reason Lucy clicks, aside from the fact that Lucille is such a great girl, is that our show is tailored to get the greatest identification. We never start off from an unbelievable premise. If the audience can accept the beginning of our show, and know that's real, like a wife being in debt or a husband trying to sneak out to a fight, then they will go along no matter how extreme the show gets."

1957

In December, Lucy and Desi offer General Tire & Rubber $6 million to purchase the old RKO Studios, where both had toiled in B movies during the 1930s and 1940s, in order to expand their thriving

Desilu facility. GT&R had bought RKO from Howard Hughes only two years previously…for $25 million! By 1960 Desilu will be grossing $20 million *a year*.

1960

Lucy and Desi, after six years of *I Love Lucy* (180 episodes) and three years of *The Lucy-Desi Comedy Hour* (13 one-hour episodes), call it quits for real, and get divorced. Lucy marries comedian Gary Morton the following year, and Desi will marry redhead Edie Hirsch in 1963, but they will remain friends and seek each other's advice for the rest of their lives. Eventually, once all those involved were deceased, Lucie Arnaz admitted her parents were the loves of each other's lives.

1960

Lucy heads east and signs on to do a Broadway musical, her first: *Wildcat*. Her personal reviews are stunning, but even though critics wrote off the show, sold-out houses proved people wanted to see Lucy live. The show folds only when Lucy is forced to leave due to emotional and physical exhaustion.

1962

Lucy returns to series television with pal Vivian Vance in *The Lucy Show*. Though her character, Lucy Carmichael, is pretty much a widowed Lucy Ricardo, audiences still love Lucy, and the series is a Top Five hit, reaching number 2 in its final season six years later. This same year, Lucy will buy out husband Desi Arnaz's share of Desilu, and become the first female head of a Hollywood studio. Her final acts as chairman, before selling the studio to Paramount in 1967 for $17 million, include greenlighting the pilots for *Star Trek* and *Mission: Impossible*.

1966	William Frawley dies. His last professional appearance was a cameo on *The Lucy Show*.
1968	Lucy changes format of her sitcom again, creating *Here's Lucy*. Her Lucy Carter character lives with her grown children, played by Lucy's real-life kids Lucie and Desi Jr. But Ball is still playing the trouble-prone, lovable, celebrity-crazy "Lucy." Audiences tune in for another six years, giving Ball a record-breaking 21-plus seasons of continually playing the same character.
1974	Lucy retires from the weekly series grind. She will continue to perform in one TV movie (1985's *The Stone Pillow*) and a handful of specials over the next decade.
1976	*LIFE* magazine publishes a special Bicentennial issue, "Remarkable American Women," featuring Lucille Ball prominently on the cover.
1977	Lucy's beloved mom, DeDe, dies. For Lucy, who had dedicated herself to keep-

ing her family close ever since her nomadic childhood, this was a major blow.

1979   Lucy's comedy partner Vivian Vance dies of cancer. She had last appeared with Lucy on the 1977 TV special *Lucy Calls the President*.

1986   On December 22, Lucy is honored with the Kennedy Center Lifetime Achievement Award, which must have somewhat eased the pain of the failure of her final sitcom, *Life with Lucy*, that fall. (After eight episodes aired in the fall of 1986, to disappointing ratings and savage reviews, the show was yanked by ABC.) Lucy was less consolable about the death of longtime husband and business partner Desi Arnaz, earlier in December. His remembrances of her for the Kennedy tribute were particularly touching. The weekend-long celebration "was the epitome—the absolute epitome," Lucy said. "I hope I never get another award, because nothing can ever top it." Her professional life from now on will consist of sporadic public appearances, usually accepting an award or honor (sorry, Lucy!), until her final appearance, as a presenter (with longtime pal Bob Hope) at the 1989 Academy Awards.

1989

Lucy dies on April 26 of a ruptured aorta. The world mourns the loss of its premiere female clown with the same ceremony and grief accorded a President, national hero, or head of state. After her death, the honors and tributes continue on a multiple basis, year after year (see previous chapter).

4

Lucy's Iconic TV Moments

The major reason we still love Lucy is that her TV series remains so darned funny, even after 55 years and numerous repetitive viewings. The Ricardos and the Mertzes—and to a lesser extent, Lucys Carmichael and Carter—have become part of our cultural heritage, part of our extended family, if you will.

I tried to limit my favorite Lucille Ball TV moments to 10. It simply can't be done. The traditional "top Lucy" episodes picked by fans are the ones that showcase Lucy, on her own, doing that fabulous slapstick she perfected on the small screen. So let's note upfront that:

Lucy filming a TV commercial while getting progressively sloshed;

Lucy learning to stomp grapes so she can appear in a neo-realistic Italian movie;

Lucy fooling Harpo Marx with his own mirror routine;

Lucy getting caught by Ricky with her foot stuck in a bucket of cement; and

Lucy performing many other slapstick moments of perfection too numerable to list here…are matchless and without peer.

I love those episodes, too, but my favorites from *I Love Lucy* tend to be the ones in which Lucy Ricardo and Ethel Mertz are pitted against Ricky and Fred, or the two couples are pitted against each other, and so on. In these episodes, the comedy comes equally out of the characters' situation and the slapstick. *The Lucy-Desi Comedy Hour*, the first two seasons (especially) of *The Lucy Show*, and, on occasion, even *Here's Lucy* offered some classic Lucy moments; those are also included.

You'll note how easy it is to picture each of the scenes described below in your mind as you read it. That's a good indication that they've become icons on their own. Here are my favorite iconic Lucy moments, in no particular order. For comparison purposes, two other (more standard) Top Ten *I Love Lucy* episode lists follow them.

1. Ethel cuts Lucy's spaghetti with a manicure scissors at the Brown Derby because Lucy is being out-stared by William Holden and freezes up while eating. (*I Love Lucy*)

2. Lucy sets her fake nose on fire and then dunks it in a cup of coffee to put it out while trying to hide from William Holden (with whom she embarrassed herself at the Brown Derby). (*I Love Lucy*)

3. Lucy and Ethel fight a losing battle with a candy conveyor belt. (*I Love Lucy*)

4. Lucy and Vivian try to fix their broken stall shower and almost drown. (*The Lucy Show*)

5. Lucy rehearses the tango with Ricky while hiding three-dozen eggs on her person. (*I Love Lucy*)

6. Ethel responds to judge Gale Gordon with "We raise chickens," after Lucy and Ricky, and Danny Thomas and TV wife Marjorie Lord, have each pointed out their children to the court. (*The Lucy-Desi Comedy Hour*)

7. "Ethel to Tillie. Ethel to Tillie." Madame Mertzola tries to raise the dead during a séance at the Ricardo's apartment in order to undo some bad juju Lucy has stirred up by reading Ricky's wrong horoscope. (*I Love Lucy*)

8. Lucy and Ethel disguise themselves as Martians for a movie publicity stunt to make money to donate to Lucy's snooty friend's charity. (*I Love Lucy*)

9. Fred, Ricky, and Lucy clown behind Ethel, getting the real applause, while Ethel grandstands singing "Shortnin' Bread" in her hometown, Albuquerque. (*I Love Lucy*)

10. The Mertzes and Ricky rehearse Lucy's trip to the hospital to have her baby. All goes well until the actual trip is necessary. (*I Love Lucy*)

11. The "baby" that Lucy has on her lap during the airplane trip home from Europe, actually a large disguised cheese that customs wouldn't allow through, "disappears," and Lucy's seatmate, also with child (the perfectly aghast Mary Jane Croft) thinks Lucy's done in the baby. (*I Love Lucy*)

12. Lucy Carmichael tries to teach an Ethel Merman look-alike (who's actually the real Merm, aiming for some privacy) to sing for a charity benefit. *(The Lucy Show)*

13. Lucy and Ethel steal John Wayne's cement-slab footprints from the Grauman's Chinese Theater forecourt (Lucy berates Ethel for getting cold feet about a "routine souvenir hunt") and get tabbed as a "frowsy redhead" and a "dishwater blonde" in the papers the next day. (*I Love Lucy*)

14. A semi-hysterical Ethel keeps Ricky occupied by babbling while Lucy (literally) flies by their L.A. hotel patio, having fallen off Cornel Wilde's patio above. (*I Love Lucy*)

15. Lucy gets Liz Taylor's huge diamond ring stuck on her finger and substitutes her hand for Liz's during a press conference. (*Here's Lucy*)

16. The substitute-hand routine was borrowed from the much funnier *I Love Lucy* second-season episode "The Handcuffs," in which Lucy, cuffed to Ricky, uses her hands to gesture for him during a performance of "Santiago Chile." It, in turn, was partially based on an episode of Lucy's radio show, *My Favorite Husband*. Not to worry though—head writer Jess Oppenheimer, and scribes Bob Carroll and Madelyn Pugh, were only plagiarizing themselves.

17. Fred and Ethel enter in bathrobes with pieces of their plaster ceiling and a chandelier on their heads as a result of the Ricardos one-night-only stand playing "El Break-o the Lease-o" upstairs from the Mertzes. (*I Love Lucy*) [Note: Watch Lucille Ball and Desi Arnaz try not to crack up at the Mertzes' entrance.]

18. Lucy and Viv try to install a TV antenna on the roof of their house. Will Lucy get stuck in the smoking chimney? (You can bet your henna rinse!) (*The Lucy Show*)

19. The Ricardos and the Mertzes get trapped in a Swiss ski hut during an avalanche and fight over the last scraps of food. (*I Love Lucy*)

20. Mrs. Trumbull tells Lucy she has a fiery temper like her red hair, and Lucy gestures at Ethel, asking, "What about her?" Ethel: "Oh, mine's as cold as her dark roots." (The best friends are fighting over a washing machine.) (*I Love Lucy*)

21. Lucy and Ethel trick the boys into thinking they're being robbed while washing dishes, working late in the back of

the restaurant where the foursome recently had dinner. This was payback for Fred and Ricky making the girls earn their keep—for not having any money to take care of the tab and just assuming Ricky and Fred would. (*I Love Lucy*)

22. Lucy, Ricky, Fred, and Ethel play hide and seek with a huge fish in their Florida hotel rooms. (*I Love Lucy*)

23. Lucy tries to get a note out (the chorus has been told to drown her out) as the Queen of the Gypsies in The Wednesday Fine Arts League's on-the-cheap production of "The Operetta." (*I Love Lucy*)

24. Lucy Carmichael, stuck for a night sleeping in the same room as best pal Vivian Bagley, and saddled with bunk beds on top of it, uses stilts to get into the top bunk. (*The Lucy Show*)

25. In Connecticut, Ethel helps Lucy rebuild the backyard barbecue, which they have taken apart during the night looking for Lucy's lost wedding ring. When Lucy, teary-eyed, calls Ethel a true friend, Ethel, ready to drop, retorts, "If I'd known this was what being a friend was for, I'd have signed up as an enemy!" (*I Love Lucy*)

The Top Ten *I Love Lucy* Episodes as chosen online at CBS.com for the *I Love Lucy 50th Anniversary Special*, broadcast on November 11, 2001.

1. "Lucy Does a TV Commercial"

2. "Job Switching" (The Candy Factory)

3. "Lucy's Italian Movie"

4. "Lucy is Enciente"

5. "L.A. at Last"

6. "Lucy and Harpo Marx"

7. "The Freezer"

8. "The Great Train Robbery"

9. "Bon Voyage (Lucy Misses the Boat to Europe)"

10. "Paris at Last"

The *TV Guide/*TV Land Top 10 (of 50) Funniest moments of *I Love Lucy* (for the full list, see the October 13, 2001 issue of *TV Guide*)

1. Vitameatavegamin.

2. Lucy's fake nose catches fire in front of Bill Holden.

3. Grape Stomping.

4. The Candy Factory.

5. Lucy gets a loving cup stuck on her head.

6. Trying out as a showgirl, Lucy's elaborate headdress trips her up going down the stairs every time.

7. Lucy smuggles a cheese home from Europe disguised as a baby.

8. As a pioneer woman, Lucy bakes an enormous loaf of bread by accident.

9. Lucy and Ethel get the latest Paris fashions (burlap sacks devised by Ricky and Fred to teach the girls a lesson).

10. Lucy needs to learn ballet in order to get into Ricky's show.

5

A Red Hair-ing

If Lucy has become an icon for our age, one of the most recognizable faces of our, or any, time, one can assume there is something unique about her face. Capable of being beautiful one minute and outlandish the next, Lucy's face was one of extremes: overarched, sophisticated eyebrows (they were in fact, not real; she'd had them shaved for one of her first movie roles, and they never grew back) framed impossibly big, blue eyes; and a cupid's bow of a mouth that took on a life of its own as Lucy reworked it with lipstick, year after year, into her 70s, meticulously creating the bow at top and full lower lip. Her pale skin served as a neat blank canvas for the rest.

Framing her entire face were ribbons, and then curls, of the most outlandishly red hair ever created. It flamed, and with it Lucy (and her career) caught fire.

Lucy's original hair color was light brown. When she first came to Hollywood, in 1933, she tried life as a blonde for a while, but found that it didn't really distinguish her from dozens of other capable wisecracking blondes who'd already staked their territory in La La Land. Of course, up until 1942 Lucy wasn't seen in color on film, so the question was somewhat of a moot point.

After she joined the MGM circle of stars, hairstylist Sidney Guilaroff chose to change Lucy's hair to a vibrant hue tinged with pink and orange called Tango Red. His explanation, from his autobiography, *Crowning Glory*, is this: "In the 1946 film *Ziegfeld Follies*, Lucy wore an apricot dress and a pompadour hairstyle, and cracked a whip over the heads of chorines in cat costumes that sparkled with sequins and jet beads. I felt she needed to stand out, so I mixed a variety of hair dyes into a henna rinse that transformed her into a shimmering golden redhead. That formula became the basis for her on-screen persona...." (Guilaroff first worked with Lucy on the 1943 musical *DuBarry Was a Lady*; her red hair was set by MGM for her first film there, 1943's *Best Foot Forward*.)

Indeed, it became Lucy's signature color. With this change, Lucy believed, her career began to take off. Critic Alexander Doty in a 1990 article in *Cinema Journal*—"The Cabinet of Lucy Ricardo: Lucille Ball's Star Image"—charged that, though Guilaroff created the color, Lucy took credit for it, "as a conscious, image-building choice," quoting Ball thusly: "When I chose that shade, things began to break for me. It gave me just the right finishing touch before the cameras."

Doty discussed Lucy's hair color as an essential part of her image: "Even if the Technicolor MGM musicals did not make Ball a movie star, they did establish a crucial element of her later star image by fetishizing her red hair...to camouflage somewhat limited singing and dancing talents with color spectacle."

It's no wonder she kept the trademark color for the rest of her life. And over the years, it became her most readily identified iconic feature.

"At the center of the Lucy phenomenon is 'Lucy,' that combination of Lucille Ball and the series of screwy redheaded heroines she infused with a life of their own. The red hair is one of the most fetishized aspects of the Lucy icon, ironic since *I Love Lucy* was, of course, in black and white," Lori Landay wrote in her 1998 essay, "Millions 'Love Lucy': Commodification and the Lucy Phenomenon."

"That women's hair color was commoditized and fetishized was certainly nothing new in the mid-1930s," Landay points out. "By choosing red hair over blonde, Ball eschewed the well-established gold-digger/dumb blonde image in favor of the unconventional, individualistic, and vibrant redhead."

Lucy was never one to hide the truth. In fact, her red hair (and the henna rinse that kept it just so) became the source of many one-liners throughout the run of *I Love Lucy* and her subsequent series. Doty affirmed, "Narrative events and dialogue references concerning red hair in the black-and-white *I Love Lucy* established her hair color as one of the central elements of Ball's star persona.... Series scripts used the artificiality of Lucy's hair color as a constant source of humor: frequent henna rinse and black root jokes, as well as farcical actions revolving around Lucy's struggles to keep her hair red, or to keep intact the secret of her red hair."

Ultimately, this led to Lucy's red hair color being so closely associated with her clowning and her screwball image that it was impossible to separate them. But such was the snug fit between star and hair color that even though the public knew it was an artifice—and that later in life, Lucy wore mostly wigs while performing or in public—she was forever branded the "wacky redhead."

6

Lucy the Icon II

Wikipedia, the online encyclopedia: "Job Switching" ("Speeeeeeed it up a little!!")—Lucy and Ethel attempt to get jobs, for which they are demonstrably unprepared. The classic candy-gobbling scene in this episode is an **American cultural icon**.

Out, November 2001 issue: In "We Love Lucy" by Bob Smith, Lee Tannen (Author of *I Loved Lucy: My Friendship with Lucille Ball*) noted that, "Lucy Ricardo is a **gay icon**. Lucy Ricardo was the underdog who was always trying to prove herself, and I think many gay men can identify with that." Smith added, "In some ways Lucy Ricardo was the perfect gay icon for the post-Stonewall generation. She wasn't a tragic victim…. (She) wasn't sharp-tongued like Bette Davis or a monster like Joan Crawford; she was beautiful and funny, and she was a comic victim of her own kooky ideas that always seemed to backfire…. But I think the main reason Lucy Ricardo is a gay icon is that *I Love Lucy* was truly romantic."

The Notable Names Database on the Web (www.nndb.com) classifies celebrities by a number of variables, then assigns them a Level of Fame, ranging from "Niche" to "Somewhat" to "Famous" to "Icon," a label afforded very few. Lucy is, of course, an **Icon**.

"When she died in 1989, she left behind a public that revered her as an **American icon**."—Lucille Ball tribute on GirlPress.com

"…It was the small screen and her ability to 'make 'em laugh' that turned [Ball] into an **influential icon** who still reverberates in the entertainment industry today."—WNET, New York's public broadcasting station, on its *American Masters* episode, "Finding Lucy."

"The show went on to become a **nostalgic icon** of American television and history. It has been estimated that over a billion people have watched *I Love Lucy*."—U.S. and European publisher Graphique de France

"If there is a more common or **beloved pop-culture icon** from late 20th-century America than Lucille Ball, I'd be hard pressed to name it."—*Austin* (Texas) *Chronicle*, August 9, 1996

"Lucille Ball and Louis Satchmo Armstrong. Two **American icons**. Both born in August, both deceased, whose talents live on…"—BroadwaytoVegas.com, an entertainment Web site [Note: Armstrong and Ball were also the number two and three icons of the past century as chosen by *Variety*. See Chapter 13 for more.]

"An icon is a human sound bite, an individual reduced to a name, a face and an idea…. If, compared with the male icons of our time, our **female icons** seem to loom larger in our culture and to cast a longer shadow, perhaps it's because in so many cases their stories have had the urgency of history in the making."—"The Age of the Female Icon" by Holly Bruback, *The New York Times*, 1996 [Note: The accompanying photo montage included Carole Lombard, Jacqueline Onassis, Doris Day, Lucille Ball, Rosa Parks, Marlene Dietrich, and Raquel Welch.]

"[*I Love Lucy*] has become such an **icon in American culture** that it's nearly impossible to imagine it [being done] in any other way."—Robert Ito, *Los Angeles* magazine, August 2003

Even the *I Love Lucy* set has acquired an iconic status. In Diana Friedman's book, *Sitcom Style* (2005), David Sackeroff, a production designer who recreated the Ricardo's apartment for a CBS special, said, "When you have **an icon like *I Love Lucy***, everyone remembers the set to look a certain way even though it may have changed." Oddly, since the show was filmed in black-and-white, he added that, "The only thing anyone who worked on the original set remembers was that they couldn't use any color on the set that would compete with Lucy's hair." Thus, as Friedman notes, "For the most part, this demand (and the limitations of black-and-white film) meant that the set, wardrobe, and props were in various shades of gray."

7

Lucy, Meet Lucy

Here's a "What were they thinking?" Lucy moment: Lucy Carter "meets" a dark-haired Lucille Ball—who is promoting the film *Mame*—during a Lucy look-alike contest.

Huh?!

On *Here's Lucy*, Ball's fourth successful prime time series, Episode #141 aired March 4, 1974. Called "Lucy Carter Meets Lucille Ball," the thin plot had Kim (Lucie Arnaz) entering a Lucille Ball look-alike contest. She doesn't make the cut. Incensed, her over-protective mother Lucy Carter (Lucille Ball) brings the matter to Lucille Ball herself ("guest star" Lucille Ball!), who insists that Carter and Kim be in the contest.

Never mind the resolution. (Did you doubt it would be a happy one?) Let's examine the reasoning behind the plot for this episode, and why it was attempted. Certainly one of the oddest Lucy episodes ever, there was likely one major reason for it going into production: Lucy herself was opening that spring in the big-budget, big-screen musical *Mame*, and the film needed all the publicity it could get. What better way to get it than by featuring a related plot on a popular half-hour prime-time sitcom? So what if the plot seems contrived (and it surely is); it doesn't matter, because the real excitement in this episode comes from the in-joke of having Lucille Ball's TV character meet Lucille Ball the STAR.

Thanks to the magic of special effects, Lucy and Lucille can co-exist in the same screen, and if anyone tuned in, that was what they were waiting to see. One can imagine her fans going, "Oh, look, isn't that marvelous! How funny! Lucy is meeting *Lucy*!"

But there's another reason the show almost works, despite itself. Lucy's iconic status was already a given in 1974. She was nearing the end of her fourth hit series and nearly a quarter century of being on TV Monday nights. It isn't likely one could find a more liked or better-known celebrity at the time. By performing in a "Lucy meets Lucy" plot, Ball was commenting on her own celebrity, giving a big WINK to the audience, and, at the same time, letting them know there was a difference between Lucy Ball and Lucy Ricardo et al.

The big irony is that the "Lucille Ball, movie star" portrayed by Lucy herself (in "serious" mode) is probably no more like the real Ball than was Lucy Carter. The film plugging was an extra; her fans would go see the film no matter what shape it was in, and that was that.

She should have known that, as a gimmick, the idea was okay, but it certainly wasn't a classic episode of TV, or even close. And it probably didn't convince anyone that Lucy was anything other than the madcap, lovable character she'd played for 25 years. In her later years, Lucy didn't like to let her fans get too close to her. She knew she looked nothing like the younger Lucy being seen many times a day on TV across the country, and didn't want them to be disappointed.

It didn't matter. Lucille Ball was destined to be remembered as Lucy. And even those fans looking at the real woman in her seventies managed to somehow see the face of a youngish, good-looking redhead, an eternal optimist who was constantly trying to make her life more exciting, and dragging us along while she did it.

Even the man who "discovered" Lucy and brought her out to Hollywood had trouble distinguishing between Lucy Ricardo and

Lucille Ball, as this revealing anecdote from Desi Arnaz's *A Book* illustrates:

One week, *I Love Lucy* came up two-and-a-half minutes short. Desi thought it would be great to get a clip of Frank Sinatra singing from the yet-to-open movie *Guys and Dolls* to fill the space (which was supposed to be an act in one of Lucy and Ethel's club shows). The movie was produced by Sam Goldwyn, who hired Lucy (at Busby Berkeley's insistence) for her first job in Hollywood back in 1933 as one of the Goldwyn Girls for the film *Roman Scandals*. Desi figured all he had to do was call Goldwyn and ask for permission. He was right, but in trying to explain to the Hollywood legend what was needed, this exchange took place:

"Well, Mr. Goldwyn, I thought perhaps I could get some film for you to fill in this two-and-a-half minutes."

"Oh, sure, but I'll tell you what," he said, "I'll do better than that. I will come over to your studio and talk on your television show with Lucy about when she came out here as a Goldwyn Girl."

"I see. Well, Mr. Goldwyn, uh...uh...thank you very much—but we can't do that."

"Why can we not do that?"

"Well, Lucy's not Lucille."

"Lucy's not Lucille?"

There followed a funny Abbott & Costello-type routine regarding the difference between Lucy [Ricardo] and Lucille [Ball]. Ultimately, Goldwyn never really got what Desi was trying to explain, and ended the conversation with, "I really don't know what it is you want, and I have to hang up, but whatever it is—you got it."

So...if the "Lucy meets Lucille" episode of *Here's Lucy* was indeed a final grace note from Ball to her fans—noting gently, "Look, I might play this wacky woman on TV, but I'm not really her."—unfortunately, for Lucy, by then it was way too late for fans to separate the two.

8

I'm an Icon, Too

"Vivian Vance is the best second banana in the business"—Mary Wickes, as quoted by Madelyn Pugh Davis in her book, *Laughing with Lucy* (2005).

Wickes was no slouch in the second-banana business herself, so that compliment from her carries a lot of weight.

When you think of television's best loved supporting character, one name always vies for the top spot: *I Love Lucy*'s Ethel Mertz, as played to perfection by Broadway actress Vivian Vance. The Academy of Television Arts and Sciences (the group that gives out the Emmy Awards) recognized this when Vance won the first Best Supporting Actress Emmy in 1953 (she was nominated three more times throughout the 1950s).

Vance was immediately beloved as best friend and confidante to the wacky Lucy Ricardo. In fact, her character was intended as the surrogate with whom the audience could identify: the more conservative best friend and neighbor, who, lacking excitement in her life, could generally be persuaded, often initially against her own good judgment, to participate in Lucy's various schemes.

She became Ethel so completely, despite misgivings—"I had a hell of a time adjusting to the identity of Ethel, especially being thought of as the wife of someone I wouldn't have married in a million years."—that she once noted, wryly, "When I die, there will be people who send flowers to Ethel Mertz."

Here are some indications that Vivian-Vance-as-Ethel-Mertz is her own icon:

- When it was revealed that Vance did not have a star on the Hollywood Walk of Fame, the Hollywood Chamber of Commerce received more than 8,000 calls in protest. (Vance got her star posthumously, in 1991).

- Vance had a play written about her, one of the few actresses to merit such an honor, with her name in the title, by John Wuchte, called *Vivian Vance Is Alive and Well and Running a Chinese Take-Out*. A meditation on the cost of fame, the off-Broadway show debuted in 1994, and is covered in detail in my book, *Lucy in Print*.

- The online encyclopedia, *The Free Dictionary*, notes that, "Vivian Vance played a significant part in the history of television. She *defined the role of second banana* [italics mine], paving the way for future female sidekicks."

- In May 2004, the TV Land series *Top Ten* focused on *TV's Wacky Neighbors*, and viewers who voted made Fred and Ethel Mertz number 9 on the list.

- In August 2004, Vance was honored in the television special *TV's Greatest Sidekicks* as "being one of the top sidekicks ever," by such actresses and peers as Bea Arthur, Valerie Harper, and Betty White. Web critic Jackie K. Cooper noted, "Lucille Ball may have been the star but Vance gave her solid support at every turn."

- Since the Internet Movie Database began tracking celebrity popularity through its STARMeter—its ranking, reports IMDb, "provides a snapshot of who's popular based on the searches of millions of IMDb users"—Vance has consistently ranked in the Top 5,000 or so (shuffling between approximately 1,800 and 5,900), not bad for a supporting character actress whose heyday was more than half a century ago.

What did Vance herself think of her *Lucy* fame? It bothered her, especially through the run of *I Love Lucy*, when people assumed she was married to William Frawley in real life. She also hated being identified as "frumpy" Ethel Mertz. After a while, she said, "You're not sure who you are—Ethel Mertz or Vivian Vance." That was a major reason Vance had it put in her *Lucy Show* contract that her character was to be named Vivian.

She eventually, via years of therapy, came to accept the fact that her association with Lucy as Ethel was a positive one, and certainly the main point on her professional résumé, the one acting job, if any, for which she'd be remembered. Vance was also shrewd enough to know that the fame Lucy bought her made it possible for her to continue working in other arenas.

"I don't think TV kept me from anything," she told *Esquire* in the mid-1970s. "My ambition never was to be a big star. I wanted to go to the store and get my money, and that was all…. What I wanted was my identity, and I got that by going to a good analyst and doing summer stock. But I wouldn't have sold out those theaters had I not been Ethel."

She ended her life in peaceful, if grudging, acceptance, acknowledging her fame had brought her every actor's dream: a commercial and the attending residuals. "That's how I've ended up on TV," she said, "selling coffee and loving it."

One Last Word: Although Vance periodically used her *I Love Lucy* fame to generate profits as a commercial spokesperson, as noted above (I'm not sure that Bill Frawley ever did) it's a shame they missed the modern era, in which famous people, dead or alive, are used to hawk almost any product.

PacifiCare Health Systems Inc. of Cypress, Calif., understands this, and launched a national marketing campaign in October 2005 for its new Medicare program. So what, you say? Well, it starred none other than the erstwhile Fred and Ethel Mertz.

Created by Deutsch Inc., the "Choice is Swell" campaign featured digital-imaging technology and film techniques "never before used in a commercial," PacifiCare reported. "Innovative production techniques combine body doubles, voice impersonators, original sets and computer-generated imagery to enable Fred and Ethel to 'speak' once more," Through the magic of Hollywood, famously cheap Fred Mertz (Frawley) and his famously exasperated wife Ethel (Vance) were used in a series of vignettes about inexpensive Medicare coverage.

According to Howard Phanstiel, PacifiCare's chairman and chief executive officer, "Fred and Ethel were expected to create a memorable message that resonates with seniors, an audience that values choice, quality and affordability.

"We are confident that the 'Choice is Swell' campaign will effectively highlight our plan's affordability and quality…. Fred and Ethel are *American icons* [italics mine] that capture the essence of a generation and its desire to get the best value for its money. After exploring numerous advertising options, we chose Fred and Ethel because of their enduring popularity and strong appeal, not only with seniors, but also with Baby Boomers and people of all ages."

9

Lucy the Icon III

Thomas Wagner, writer, *American Masters'* "Finding Lucy": "She is extraordinarily consistent in her portrayal of [the Lucy] character."

Desi Arnaz (in 1957): "I think there are several reasons [for our success]. For one thing, we've always tried to come up with new approaches, so people won't get tired of seeing us do the same old things. We've got real people on our show. They live like normal human beings; the audience can identify itself with them. The situations may get pretty wacky, but they start on a logical premise. We've got a show with four underdogs. One week, Lucy will get the worst of it, the next time it might be Ricky, the next time Fred or Ethel…. One of the big reasons for the show's success is Lucy. She is the greatest."

Alexander Doty: "…Ball realized that the construction of her television character was the result of a series of denials: of glamour, high style, wealth, wit, and independence, that is, of certain key elements in her film image."—writing in *Cinema Journal*, 1990

Gale Gordon: "Lucille didn't care about messing herself up. A lot of stars of her stature wouldn't do physical comedy because they were afraid they'd get their hair messed up or they'd look bad. I remember once she fell into a vat of green dye. She came out with not only her hair green but everything was green!"

Charles Higham, author: Jess Oppenheimer "drew some elements from [*The Baby Snooks Show*] for the 'Lucy' concept.... The characters Fanny [Brice] and Lucy played were essentially alike—both were very childlike."—writing in *Lucy: The Real Life of Lucille Ball*, 1987

Vivian Vance: "[When I travel], people keep coming up to me and chattering away. They can't understand why I don't know what they're saying because they've heard 'me' speaking German or French or Italian." (*I Love Lucy* was dubbed into 52 languages.)

Molly Haskell, film critic: "Lucy may surrender in the final clinch, but she is no 'surrendered' wife. In the final analysis, Lucy is a fireball who treads a fine line between independence and submission, the stay-at-home wife who wouldn't."

Erma Bombeck, humorist: "Lucy, I've been trying to think what set you apart from the Harriet Nelsons, the Donna Stones, the June Cleavers, and Maude, Ann Romano, and Mother Walton, and you know what I decided? You were real. Yes, you were. With all the exaggeration, the clowning, and the contrivances, the best any of us could hope for was a bit of Lucy's perspective. I guess all I really wanted to say is, that when the pages of women's history are being written, if the name Lucy Ricardo is not there, it will not reflect the heroine of 70 million housewives of the 1950s.

"What did you do? You saved our sanity."—part of a 1970s *Good Morning, America* tribute

Gale Gordon: "For comedy to be good, it has to be played straight. And again, the greatest example of this is Lucy Ball. No matter how wild the shows were that we did, no matter how bizarre the situations were, they were never played as if they were funny. They were played like serious incidents of ordinary everyday life. And that's why they are terribly funny and are still considered classic comedies."

Vivian Vance: "Have you ever noticed that with all the sharp words Lucy and I exchange during an episode, we always end up friends? That's one of the secrets of our successful formula. The audience has come to realize, perhaps subconsciously, that every show is going to have a happy ending. The script never lets any of us really hurt one another."

Joyce Millman, writing in *The New York Times*, October 14, 2001: "As a clown, Ball was a radical, powerful figure. It was as if she was daring you to think it was unseemly for a woman to put on a putty nose or a fright wig and throw herself into a joke with body and soul…. Ball used her full-throttle clowning to assert her character's cool confidence in herself. Lucy Ricardo was kooky but she was no dumbbell. Her schemes were creative, impeccably logical, and courageous."

Lucille Ball: "I'm not funny. What I am is brave."

(On producer and head writer Jess Oppenheimer, and writers Bob Carroll and Madelyn Pugh): "I love them dearly, I appreciate them daily, I praise them hourly, and I thank God for them every night."

(On creating her "Lucy" character): "A kind of everywoman, a very basic American person…. I wanted [someone] middle-American, a housewife worrying about all the things housewives all over the world worry about. Domestic situations everyone could understand…just *slightly* exaggerated…. It didn't occur to me until much later that Vivian Vance and I were doing Laurel & Hardy. Somebody told me and I said, "Oh? *Yeah!*""

(On the "new realism in TV comedy" circa the early to mid-1970s): "That's a whole new trend I could never embrace. No one would ever accept it from me. I would lose the fans that I have. And I've been passed down from generation to generation."

(On her comedy): "There has to be knowledge of how to do physical things...without hurting yourself. There's no way to try to make someone funny. There's no way to tell people about timing.... I've had to believe things that were childlike. If I had to bake a loaf of bread that was literally thirteen feet long, I believed it."

—American Film Institute Seminar, 1984

10

TV Guide Weighs In

If Lucille Ball's face *has* been seen by more people than any other face in the history of the human race, part of her face becoming a recognizable icon is due to her numerous appearances on the cover of *TV Guide*. Like *I Love Lucy*, *TV Guide*—a weekly, digest-sized magazine that offered TV listings, a bit of news and gossip, and features on the medium's favorite stars—was a success right out of the gate with its first national issue on April 3, 1953. But was it because that first cover featured Lucille Ball and her "$50 Million Baby" (Desi Arnaz Jr. had just been born, to the biggest storm of publicity in the still-young medium of TV)? Perhaps.

TV Guide, which for a long time was the best-selling magazine in the country (at its peak, the magazine had more than twenty million weekly readers, becoming an icon of its own), supported Lucy ever after, putting her on more covers than any other star: thirty-four by its own reckoning in a special 2002 issue on its fifty greatest covers.

Actually, it's forty-four covers:

—Nine extra covers were created in October 2001 to honor *I Love Lucy*'s fiftieth anniversary that year. (*TV Guide* counted the 2001 set as one in its tally of thirty-four.) Eight of the covers, each with a different iconic *I Love Lucy* picture, sold on the newsstands in October 2001. A bonus cover featuring Lucy, Ricky, Fred and Ethel could only be purchased online.

—Lucy's two most recent appearances were on the August 5, 2005 and October 9, 2005 covers. Lucy and Desi Arnaz are pictured in a banner at the top of the August 5 issue announcing a special *TV Guide* trivia quiz. Craig Hamrick, my editor, and the writer who co-edits, with me, the books in the TV Tidbits series (of which this is one), wrote the quiz. October 9 was the final digest-size issue of *TV Guide*, and to celebrate its transformation into a standard-size magazine, the editors picked nine classic covers and recreated them with modern TV stars (each of the nine covers has the original inset within it). For Lucy, they picked the grape-stomping cover (one of the eight from the fiftieth anniversary celebration) and recreated it with country music/sitcom star Reba McIntyre.

Lucy died in 1989, and starting in 1993, with *TV Guide*'s fortieth anniversary, the magazine has consistently celebrated the redheaded clown in special issues and "Best-of" lists that reinforce her iconic status. Here are some of the highlights.

40th Anniversary Issue, April 17, 1993

TV Guide editors picked the "All-Time Best TV" in different categories, and Lucy scored a trifecta: *I Love Lucy* was chosen the best sitcom of the 1950s ("Why not *The Honeymooners*? Here's the short answer: Lucille Ball.") Lucy was also chosen Best Comic Actress of the 1950s ("...an elastic-faced, husky-voiced calamity-prone screwball with a bow-tie mouth, wide blue eyes, hair the color of steamed carrots") and All-Time Best Comic Actress: "Every comedic actress owes a debt to Lucy—she did it all first...with a gift for making the outrageous believable. She was America's television comic genius."

The 100 Most Memorable Moments in TV History, June 29, 1996

Mixing news (the moon-shot, the JFK assassination, O.J., Princess Di) and classic TV series episodes, Lucy clocked in at an enviable number two (Armstrong on the moon was number one) with the candy-factory conveyor belt classic from the episode "Job Switching." It was accompanied by a picture of Lucy and Ethel (Vivian Vance) trying to wrap chocolates in vain. "Classic slapstick: the chaotic crowning moment of *I Love Lucy*," said *TV Guide*.

The 100 Greatest Episodes of All Time, June 28, 1997
TV Guide and cable channel TV Land ranked these shows. Lucy is represented by the "Italian Movie" episode in which she has to learn how to stomp grapes, at Number 18, "a vat of fun, stirred up by Ball's inimitable, extravagant flair for slapstick"; and at Number 2 for her turn at trying to break into showbiz by becoming spokesperson for a new product: Vitameatavegamin: "Ball builds the mirth to a riotous climax."

45th Anniversary Celebration, April 4, 1998
Lucy is one of "45 People Who Made a Difference." *TV Guide* noted, "More than any other comedian, Lucille Ball is responsible for the modern sitcom…peerless clowning…comic genius." The first national cover of *TV Guide* (with Lucy and Desi Jr. on it), plus a classic "breathtaking pose" from 1957, the final season of *I Love Lucy*, are chosen as two of the forty-five best *TV Guide* covers, "the most coveted thirty-seven-and-a-half square inches in entertainment journalism." Lucy and Ethel are also pictured in a fashion round-up, wearing their infamous Paris "originals."

The 50 Funniest TV Moments of All Time, January 23, 1999
Again in tandem with TV Land, *TV Guide* picked the candy-wrapping scene from "Job Switching" as the twelfth funniest moment, and Lucy's Vitameatavegamin spiel as moment number 7. Lucy shared the cover with Carol Burnett and Jerry Seinfeld.

TV's 50 Greatest Characters Ever!, October 16, 1999
TV Land aired them in a broadcast special the same week; Lucy Ricardo was Number 3, behind the ever-deserving *Honeymooner* Ed Norton (Art Carney) and the inexplicably chosen list-topper, obnoxious Louie DePalma (Danny DeVito) of *Taxi*. Noted *TV Guide*, "So many of the most cherished moments in TV comedy have Lucy Ricardo in them. And just a few words bring them clearly to mind, because they've become a part of our culture.... Lucy is the medium's DNA. Her uncanny and exuberant instincts for slapstick shaped everything that followed. Let's face it: any comic actor on TV today, male or female, who claims not to have been influenced by Lucy/Lucille is lying through his or her teeth."

TV's All-Time Greatest, January 1, 2000 (Canadian *TV Guide*)
The Canadian edition's pick for all-time greatest TV star was, of course, Lucy ("She demanded the best writers, directors and co-stars. Most of all, though, she demanded of herself. Every ounce of her comic inspiration was the result of gallons of perspiration.") *I Love Lucy* was chosen the greatest TV show ("Other sitcoms have pushed TV's comedy envelope, but it was *I Love Lucy* that established it in the first place."). And Lucy Ricardo was the number two greatest TV character: "What is it that made four generations fall hopelessly in love with Lucy (Lucille Ball)? Guts. We all wish we had her kind of moxie.... But there was also a vulnerability to Lucy that kept her from ever seeming shrewish or shallow."

Greatest Shows of All Time, May 4, 2002 (Celebrating *TV Guide*'s 50th Anniversary)
I Love Lucy came in at number two, sandwiched between *Seinfeld* and *The Honeymooners*. "Loving Lucy still comes so very easily," reported *TV Guide*. "Brilliantly polished in its frantic hilarity, *Lucy* got there first and did what it did—and what so many others have tried to do—best. The legendary troupe of Lucille Ball, Desi Arnaz,

Vivian Vance and William Frawley set the standard for wacky antics, harebrained schemes, domestic humor and outrageous shtick, pretty much inventing TV comedy on the spot…. We watch *I Love Lucy* for the same reasons audiences did five decades ago: to see a genius—a true American original—at work and play. [Ball's] shenanigans with Vance are echoed in just about every dynamic duo in TV history."

Our 50 Greatest Covers of All Time, June 15, 2002

Taken chronologically, the list begins with the magazine's first national cover, featuring Lucy and her baby, Desi Jr. Soon after that comes Lucy's first solo appearance on the cover, a classic portrait of Lucy backed by her own profile, in shadow (April 23, 1954). Moving a bit further ahead is the famous Lucy jumping cover, taken by Philippe Halsman, who, it is claimed, "had Lucy jumping for three hours, and not once did she complain." (Halsman always asked his subjects to jump for him.) The cover was dated September 29, 1962, and heralded Lucy's return to weekly television in *The Lucy Show*. In crowning Ball their all-time cover appearance champ, *TV Guide* noted, "She was such an amazing clown, we sometimes forgot she was also such a beauty. Ball went from bombshell to grande dame, but she never relinquished her crown as the all-time queen of comedy."

50 Things to Love About TV, December 14, 2002

Resident *TV Guide* critic Matt Roush picked his favorite things about the tube, in no particular order. "Vitameatavegamin" was number 30, pictured with a besotted Lucy Ricardo. Roush noted, it "cures what ails you, every time you watch. If Lucille Ball is our favorite female clown, this hysterical descent into slow-building tipsiness is her most cherished routine."

The 100 Most Memorable Moments, December 5, 2004
Eight years after its first "100 Greatest Moments" list, *TV Guide* went back to the well for this list, which was also spotlighted on TV Land in five special episodes. "Job Switching" (aka "The Candy Factory") landed at Number 9 on the list (it was number two the first time around). This time, another classic episode also made the list: at Number 59 was "Lucy Goes to the Hospital," in which "Lucy shows that when it comes to breaking comic ground and making brilliant slapstick, it's all in the delivery."

11

Laughter and Lucy

With respect to Lucille Ball and the laughter she has brought into our lives, most would agree that she was, simply, capable of being extremely funny. Laughter is the response to something funny having happened or been said, and it's obvious that, going on 55 years, Lucy and her television cohorts (most especially her first husband Desi Arnaz, and *I Love Lucy* co-stars Vivian Vance and William Frawley) still deliver the goods. This suggests the essence of Lucy's legacy and somewhat explains why she's become an icon: we love the people who make us laugh. And who has made us laugh more than Lucy?

But laughter is now thought to be so much more than a mere "Ha, ha, ha," making Lucy's legacy that much more significant. Consider that many health professionals now believe the following:

Laughter works to reduce stress. Unchecked, as many have long suspected, stress will take its toll on the immune system, increase the number of blood platelets (which can clog the arteries) and raise blood pressure, the Discovery Network reports: "When we laugh, natural killer cells—which destroy tumors and viruses—increase, along with Gamma-interferon (a disease-fighting protein), T-cells (important for our immune system) and B-cells (which make disease-fighting antibodies)." Our blood pressure is lowered, and more oxygen gets into the blood, which also encourages healing. In addition, laughter is a now being touted as a **vital coping mecha-**

nism that helps us deal with humiliation, embarrassment, pain, and suffering.

The study of laughter is now a medicinal discipline. There's even a group called the Association for Applied and Therapeutic Humor (AATH). Established in 1988, its mission is "To advance the understanding and application of humor and laughter for their positive benefits."

The AATH describes therapeutic humor as "any intervention that promotes health and wellness by stimulating a playful discovery, expression, or appreciation of the absurdity or incongruity of life's situations." Very few things do that better than *I Love Lucy* and other classic sitcoms.

Laughter can help the heart. In March 2005, a team of University of Maryland School of Medicine researchers, led by Dr. Michael Miller, released the results of a study which showed for the first time that laughter is linked to the healthy function of blood vessels.

Nobel Prize-nominated doctors and scientists Patrick and Gael Crystal Flanagan, assert that "Scientists have found that **laughter is a form of internal jogging** that exercises the body and stimulates the release of beneficial brain neurotransmitters and hormones. Positive outlook and laughter is actually good for our health."

Finally, Norman Cousins, author of *Anatomy of an Illness*, wrote: "Laughter may or may not activate the endorphins or enhance respiration, as some medical researchers contend. What seems clear, however, is that **laughter is an antidote to apprehension and panic**."

Cousins also refers to laughter as "a form of jogging for the innards," and Dr. Ellen K. Rudolph, a Williamsburg, Virginia-based psychologist, agrees: "Did you know that a good belly laugh gives you the same benefits as an aerobic workout?" she asks. Now you do. Dr. Sushil Bhatia, of Framingham, Mass., "meets once a week with his employees to get them to laugh," Bhatia told *Good Morning America* in April, 2005. "The whole idea is to help people relax and let their things go," Bhatia said. "And their minds can open up to things. That's what laughter does…. Laughter is the shortest form of meditation, because while you're laughing you cannot think of anything else."

What happens when you meditate on Lucy? Think of her glorious Vitameatavegamin spiel. The corners of the mouth begin to curl up. You remember how she gets progressively plastered tasting the potion for the TV audience. "It's so tasty, too!" I'm already picturing Lucy, by this time fully enamored of the "health tonic," (i.e., drunk). She's having a problem using the spoon to ingest the liquid from the bottle, so she places the spoon on the table before her and pours the bottle over it. Bet you're smiling right now. Go ahead. Find the cassette or DVD. Put it on and laugh all over again.

That's one of the secrets of Lucy's success. She was an actress, first and foremost, and she was the first to tell anyone that she wasn't inherently funny. And, in truth, people that knew her affirm that off-screen, she was quite a serious person. But decades of training in Hollywood, via B pictures and friends like comic geniuses Harold Lloyd and Buster Keaton, not to mention a cheering section that included Orson Welles (who thought Lucy was the best comedienne in Hollywood) gave Lucy the confidence and fearlessness to be able to try anything for the sake of comedy.

That, coupled with the "Lucy" character's genuine, often childlike enthusiasm for just about anything—especially about her chances of getting into show business—created a character (and by "Lucy" we refer not just to Lucy Ricardo, but also Lucy Carmichael, Lucy Carter, and even grandma Lucy Barker) that was endearing to television audiences.

Lucy was so real and genuine; we felt we knew her from the opening gate (as evidenced by *I Love Lucy*'s meteoric rise to the top of the Nielsen ratings charts). And we followed her through zany adventure on top of zany adventure. We'd probably never get a chance to work on a candy assembly line, or stomp grapes in a New Wave Italian movie, or be a showgirl in a Hollywood movie, but we could identify with Lucy's nervousness about screwing up in such a position, which she often did. She was human, and we loved her, flaws and all.

One of the reasons we could identify, of course, was her loyal best friend and neighbor, Ethel Mertz (Vance). Ethel was our portal into Lucy's adventures, so to speak, the elder and more conservative of the duo, but someone who seems to be envious of Lucy's constant scheming. (Why else would she join in ninety-nine percent of the time?) Ethel is sometimes the voice of reason, the one saying, "Lucy, you're not gonna [fill in the blank]" but who inevitably gets pulled into Lucy's scheme. And we get pulled in with her. After all, there is that reflected glory Ethel (and we) receive by investing in Lucy's schemes. And we, as does Ethel, always forgive Lucy in the end, precisely because we know that, despite what may have happened, there wasn't an evil thought underneath that hennaed hair.

Thanks to the glorious technology of cable TV and DVD, we now need not suffer a moment of the day without a Lucy fix, if we so desire. Of course, we all have our own lives to lead, so that might not be the most prudent path. Catch Lucy when you really need her, and revel in her boundless energy, her juvenile behavior in pursuit of some very adult goals, the way she refused to be locked up in the house or categorized as a mere housewife, the loyal friend and wife she was. And when you can't actually sit down and watch Lucy, thinking about her antics will suffice...at least until the next time...and remember: watching Vitameatavegamin, if not actually imbibing it, you really can "spoon your way to health!"

12

A Clown for the Ages

Lucy's Q Score Tops Dead Celebrity List

What is a "Q score"? For forty years, Marketing Evaluations, Inc. of Manhasset, N.Y., has been measuring performers' likeability quotient, and advertisers, producers, directors, and other showbiz folk have been using the scores to decide whether they want to use a performer in any given project. "Q Scores reflect the degree to which a performer/personality is 'liked' by the people who are familiar with that performer/personality," explains Steven Levitt, president of Marketing Evaluations. On August 12, 2005, the company's most recent survey, of deceased celebrities, was released. It placed Lucille Ball squarely on top of those most missed by the public with a 52 Q score (followed closely by Bob Hope with a 51 score and John Wayne at 48).

A Q score of 19 is considered the likeability minimum, whether a celebrity is dead or alive.

Lucy "has topped past 'Dead Q' lists as her comedies seemingly live forever on television," said Levitt, adding, perhaps unnecessarily, "What is there not to like about Lucy?" According to the Web site Digital Squeeze, "Marketing Evaluations extracts its data from the responses of 1,453 adults who replied to a mailed questionnaire asking whether they recognized a celebrity's name, and then whether they'd rank that particular celebrity as being among their 'favorites.' The respondents were taken from a national sample of approximately 2,500 people who agreed to participate in the company's national consumer panel."

If Q scores measure a performer's staying power, as Marketing Evaluations maintains, then Lucy remains more popular with the public than many current stars. Her Q score puts her well above the average, and the only other stars consistently attaining high Qs are Tom Hanks (with a Q of 56), Bill Cosby (the highest Q ever attained, 71), Julia Roberts, and Sean Connery.

13

Lucy the Icon IV

Variety, the trade magazine that coined words such as *boffo* (outstanding), *oater* (a Western), and *prexy* (studio or company president) celebrated a century of reporting on show business in October 2005. To mark the occasion, it published a special issue, including a list of the top one hundred "Entertainment Icons of the Century." (We assume the magazine means the twentieth century, though technically its anniversary covers the years 1905 to 2005.) *Variety* executive editor Steven Gaydos noted, "It seemed only natural to celebrate 100 of the people who gave us something to talk about."

Only the Top Ten icons were ranked. Lucy came in at number three, behind the Beatles and Louis Armstrong. The rest of the Top Ten, in order, were Humphrey Bogart, Marlon Brando, Charlie Chaplin, James Dean, Marilyn Monroe, Mickey Mouse, and Elvis Presley.

Not so coincidentally, in a section of the issue headlined "TV Titans," Desi Arnaz is number two, thanks to his innovative approach to the sitcom: live audience, three cameras, filmed for preservation (and reruns)—let's just say it: without Arnaz, the sitcom as we know it today would not exist.

Variety used the following criteria to select its icons:

- Is the individual universally recognized?
- Commercial and creative impact.

- Social/political impact and significance.

- Degree to which the figure changed his or her field.

- Number of imitators.

- Familiarity of name.

- Endurance.

- Honors.

- Variety of media in which the figure worked.

- Is he or she on a T-shirt?

- Scope of creative works he or she inspired.

The magazine polled its own editors, the entertainment community, and its online readers in order to be able to separate those who have made an impact from those who are actually iconic in stature. Gaydos and fellow editors Carole Horst and Steve Chagollan explained, in their introduction to the list, that, "Some of the greatest figures in entertainment history changed the way we think about and relate to their art form and our world. But they weren't icons." Others (like Betty Grable, for example) may have been icons for their time, but did not endure, for various reasons; were icons in their own right but outshone by those on the list; or have not yet stood the test of time and may yet become icons.

Of Lucy herself, *Variety* noted, "The red hair, the giant eyes, the rubber face: Those were the physical tools that Lucille Ball used to ply her comic craft so expertly. In the process of trying to make people laugh, she also stole their hearts…. The depth of feeling for Ball spoke to the power of the medium she helped popularize…. Viewers around the world formed an intimate bond with the comedienne, thinking of her not as a star, like Bogart or Bacall, but as part of their extended family who dropped by on Monday nights."

And fifty-five years later, we still identify with Lucy (and Ricky, Fred, and Ethel), and welcome a drop-by via TV. Her legacy as an icon of mirth is a never-ending supply of laughter and happiness.

Afterword

In the first years of the new millennium, we were struck with terror, horror, and heartbreak, in place of the bright future we all hoped would be waiting for us. There are few, if any, cures, for the loss of a loved one, or of those heroes who've fought for our freedoms on so many fronts.

But I can tell you this: When my mother was dying of cancer, one of the great joys I had was spending time alone with her, sometimes quietly enjoying television together (she loved *MacGyver* and *The Golden Girls*)…except when we watched *I Love Lucy*, and *laughed out loud*.

That's when I first really started to believe in the healing power of laughter. As we observed Lucy fuss with her putty nose—in a doomed attempt to convince William Holden she was *not* the woman who dumped a tray-full of pies on him at The Brown Derby earlier that day—my mom burst out laughing, noting she'd forgotten how truly funny these episodes were. For several moments, she'd also totally forgotten how sick she was, and her face took on a glow that was generally missing by that time.

I am forever grateful for those moments, and for Lucy. And so are the millions of others for whom she's done the same thing: brought them out of the terror of the real world, if only for an instant, and made them smile, or laugh.

Helen Itria wrote in 1976, on the occasion of Lucy's twenty-fifth anniversary in television, "The world not only loves Lucy. The world, as it is today, needs her very much." And the world of today needs her even more.

Appendix: Honoring Lucy

Lucille Ball, during her lifetime and after, was awarded just about every honor an entertainer (and human being) could receive. These included four Emmy Awards plus a TV Academy Governor's Award (its highest honor); the first Golden Globe given for television achievement, in 1955, plus the Cecil B. DeMille Award from the Hollywood Foreign Press Association (the people who bring you the Golden Globes; again, it's the group's highest honor); the Kennedy Center Lifetime Achievement Award; and the Women in Film Lucy Award. WIF, in fact, further honored Lucy by naming an award after her (the 2005 recipients were *Will & Grace*'s Debra Messing and Megan Mullally).

Lucy was in the first group of people inducted into the Television Academy Hall of Fame, in 1984 (as the only woman, her fellow inductees included Milton Berle, Paddy Chayefsky, Norman Lear, Edward R. Murrow, William S. Paley, and David Sarnoff); husband Desi Arnaz and their show *I Love Lucy* followed her several years later. It remains the only television series thus honored to date.

She has two stars on the Hollywood Walk of Fame (one for television and one for films). She's been honored with two postage stamps since her passing. Very few celebrities have even one. New Millennium fever prompted a number of awards for "best of the century" (the Twentieth Century), and Lucy was on or at the top of any list involving popular people or personalities or entertainers.

Perhaps the most significant of these was The *Time* 100, dubbed by the weekly magazine as "The most important people of the [Twentieth] century.

Lucy, of course, was one of the 20 Artists & Entertainers chosen for the honor. There were four other categories, such as Leaders & Revolutionaries, and Builders & Titans, each also with 20 people. *Time* published five special issues that year, and Lucy was one of four entertainers chosen to grace the cover of the Artists & Entertainers issue—the others being Picasso, Steven Spielberg, and Bob Dylan—in a special color portrait by Al Hirschfeld, who'd drawn Lucy many times since the 1940s.

Of Lucy, *Time* noted, "The first lady of comedy brought us laughter as well as emotional truth. No wonder everybody loved Lucy....Guided by Ball's comic brilliance, *I Love Lucy* developed the shape and depth of great comedy. Lucy's quirks and foibles—her craving to be in showbiz, her crazy schemes that always backfired, the constant fights with the Mertzes—became as particularized and familiar as the face across the dinner table....At its peak, in 1952-53, it averaged an incredible 67.3 rating, meaning that on a typical Monday night, more than two-thirds of all homes with TV sets were tuned to Lucy.

"Ball's dizzy redhead with the elastic face and saucer eyes was the model for scores of comic TV females to follow. She and her show, moreover, helped define a still nascent medium....*I Love Lucy* was unmistakably a television show, and Ball the perfect star for the small screen. 'I look like everybody's idea of an actress,' she once said, 'but I feel like a housewife.' Sid Caesar and Jackie Gleason were big men with larger-than-life personas; Lucy was one of us."

Maybe that best explains why we love Lucy after all these years: the character of "Lucy" was one of us, and the actress playing her never pretended to be anything more or less. When we rooted for her to succeed, or laughed at her misfires, it was the laughter of recognition, of that part of Lucy that we saw, and continue to see, in ourselves. Lucy allowed us to laugh at our precarious human condi-

tion, and we honor her to this day, an icon of optimism and happiness in a world too often lacking the same.

Further Reading

Ball of Fire, 2003, Stefan Kanfer

The I Love Lucy Book, 1985, Bart Andrews

Laughs, Luck and Lucy, 1996, Jess Oppenheimer

Love, Lucy, 1997, Lucille Ball

Loving Lucy: An Illustrated Tribute to Lucille Ball, 1982, Bart Andrews and Thomas J. Watson

The Lucille Ball Quiz Book, 2004, Michael Karol

Lucille: The Life of Lucille Ball, Kathleen Brady, 2001

Lucy A to Z: The Lucille Ball Encyclopedia, Third Edition, 2004, Michael Karol

Lucy in Print, 2003, Michael Karol

Madcaps, Screwballs and Con Women: The Female Trickster in American Culture, 1998, Lori Landay

Sitcom Queens: Divas of the Small Screen, 2006, Michael Karol

The TV Guide TV Book, 1992, Ed Weiner and the Editors of *TV Guide*

About the Author

I graduated from college with a Masters in Communications, and it seemed only prudent to communicate, so I did, becoming a magazine writer and editor in New York City. After a quarter-century in publishing, I landed my dream job: as Copy Chief at *Soap Opera Weekly* I am mandated to watch TV…every day!

I've lately specialized in writing about showbiz topics and interviewed many celebrities, including Susan Lucci, Denise Nickerson, Doris Singleton, Phyllis Hyman, Jane Connell, David Hedison, and Johnny "Guitar" Watson, plus behind-the-scenes movers and shakers like *Wonderfalls* creator Bryan Fuller, *House, M.D.*'s creator and executive producer, David Shore, and Lucille Ball's personal secretary, Wanda Clark.

In 2001, I wrote my first book, focusing on the first TV star to leave a major impression on me, via that little box in the living room: Lucille Ball. The widespread acclaim for *Lucy A to Z: The Lucille Ball Encyclopedia*, convinced me there were lots of other boomers who wanted to read about television, movies, and the celebrities they watched growing up.

At *Computer Shopper*, in 1996, I began working with talented *Dark Shadows* author Craig Hamrick, also a fine photographer (my author's photo is his work), and the result is the book series (and Web site) TV Tidbits. Go to www.TVTidbits.com for more information.

My other books include *Kiss Me, Kill Me*, featuring Craig's atmospheric photos; *Lucy in Print*, published in September 2003; my first TV Tidbits book, *Funny Ladies: Sitcom Queens*, in March 2004, and, later that year, *The Lucille Ball Quiz Book*. *The ABC Movie of the Week Companion* was my third contribution to our ongoing series. This book is the fourth, and the first in our new TV Tidbits Icon Series.

To read more about Lucille Ball, my books, and other pop culture ramblings, visit my Web site at www.Sitcomboy.com.

978-0-595-37951-4
0-595-37951-6

Printed in the United States
53894LVS00001B/86

9 780595 379514